Christmas

at

Bethlehem

GULCH

AN "OLD WEST" CHILDREN'S MUSICAL
ABOUT THE COMING OF THE SAVIOR

Created by Pam Andrews

Arranged by John DeVries

lillenas
PUBLISHING COMPANY

lillenas.com

Cast

Miss Diane

Doug

Dean

Cookie

Robert

Cassie

Mitch

Suzie

Speck—Shepherd 1

Buck—Shepherd 2

Rory—Shepherd 3

Shep

Angels 1, 2, 3 & 4 (Solos—non-speaking)

Sheep 1

Sheep 2

Sheep 3

Sheep 4

Mary (non-speaking)

Joseph (non-speaking)

Kid 1

Contents

Christmas at Bethlehem Gulch Overture

includes
Bethlehem Shepherds
Baa Baa Better Believe

Arr. by John DeVries

CD: 2 *Scene 1 begins (page 8)

Scene 1*
(During the Overture)

(The CHOIR *enters as visitors to Bethlehem Gulch at the beginning of the Overture.* MISS DIANE, COOKIE, DEAN, *and* DOUG *enter from stage right and stage left to center stage.)*

MISS DIANE: Cookie? Is the grub ready?

COOKIE: Shore thing, Miss Diane. Stews on the fire and it's lookin' mm-mm good!

DOUG: I got on my new boots, Miss D.

DEAN *(spits in his hands and wipes his hair)*: Yep, I just slicked down my hair. Don't I look nice?

MISS DIANE: Yep, y'all look like a million bucks in your fancy church goin' duds. *(horn honks)* I hear the bus horn a honkin'! The busload of kids is in Heavenly Hollow. They'll be here any minute now.

DEAN: Hope things go better this time, Miss D.

DOUG: Yep, many more o' those refunds and we'll be outta business.

DEAN: Seems like kids nowadays wanna ride them there horses and rope them there steers.

DOUG: Yep, nobody wants to sheer sheep wool nowadays. Too itchy a job, I reckon.

MISS DIANE: Keep yer chin up. The Good Lord'll take care of us. There's just got to be some youngins out there that want to spend the night at a sheep ranch.

COOKIE: I hope yer right, Miss D. Cause the grub's gettin' mighty scarce.

MISS DIANE: Look, here they come!

*(*CHOIR *enters down the aisle. Some of the children could even arrive on a pretend school bus. As the* CHOIR *enters,* MISS DIANE *shakes hands with the kids and greets them.)*

MISS DIANE: Howdy, everyone! Howdy! Nice to meet ya! Come right on in! Store your gear any 'ol where. Grab a bail of hail or an ole' stump and have a seat. Welcome to Bethlehem Gulch! You're gonna have a mess of fun. Now, hold on! This is gonna be a rough and rowdy ride! Welcome, everybody! Welcome!!!! *(Overture ends)*

(Music begins)

Christmas at Bethlehem Gulch

with
Home on the Range

Words and Music by
PAM ANDREWS
Arr. by John DeVries

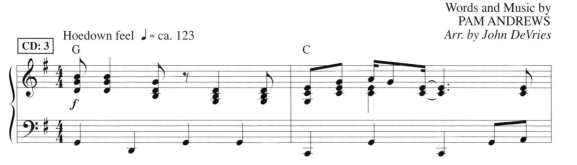

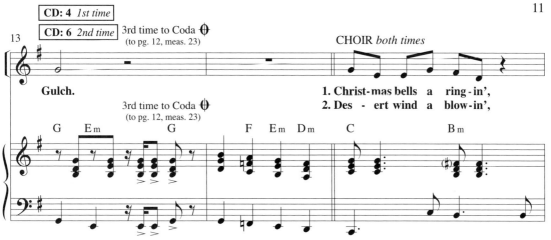

CD: 4 *1st time*
CD: 6 *2nd time* | 3rd time to Coda (to pg. 12, meas. 23)

CHOIR *both times*

Gulch.

3rd time to Coda (to pg. 12, meas. 23)

1. Christ-mas bells a ring-in',
2. Des - ert wind a blow-in',

All the folks are sing-in', Joy He is a bring-in',
Stars, they are a glow-in', Hearts they are a know-in',

Je - sus Christ is born, On this Christ - mas

12

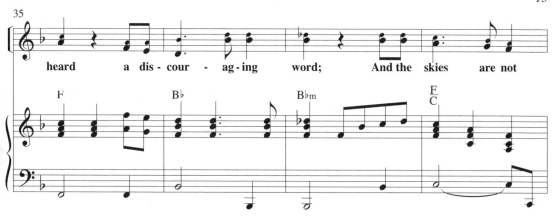

heard a dis - cour - ag - ing word; And the skies are not

CD: 9
Hoedown feel ♩ = ca. 123

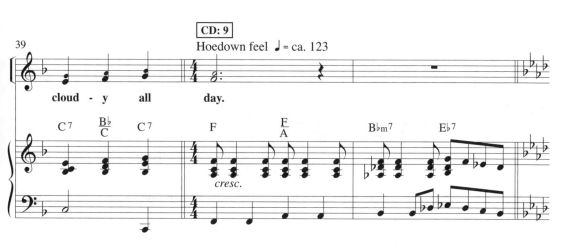

cloud - y all day.

cresc.

MISS DIANE
f
Wel - come, wel - come, come on in,

CHOIR *unis.*
f
Wel - come, wel - come, how - dy one and all;___

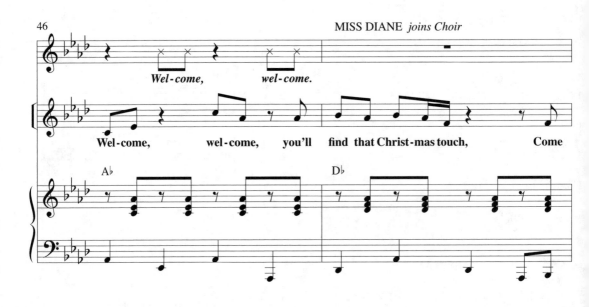

*A live solo instrument can be used to play the vocal melody.

Scene 2

(SUZIE, MITCH, CASSIE, and ROBERT enter down the center aisle meeting MISS DIANE center stage. CHILDREN make comments such as, "I'm so glad we're here," or "This place looks awesome," etc. MISS DIANE greets the children, shaking hands with MITCH. ROBERT moves to stand in the shadows behind a tree or simply stands alone away from the group.)

MISS DIANE: Howdy, kids!

KIDS: Howdy!

MITCH: I'm Mitchell and we're the First Church Kid's Choir.

MISS DIANE: Nice to make your acquaintance, Mitch. I'm Miss Diane, but the folks around the gulch call me Miss D. What a fine group of youngins! *(motions to the choir)*

MITCH: We wanted to do something really special this year for our Christmas Party and Suzie *(gestures to SUZIE)* found your ranch online.

SUZIE: Howdy. *(shakes hands with MISS DIANE)*

MISS DIANE: Well howdy right back at ya, Suzie. *(to CASSIE)* And what's your name, little lady?

CASSIE: I'm Cassie Lee and I'm from New York City.

DOUG & DEAN: NEW YORK CITY???

COOKIE: Oh no, we got ourselves an 'ole "City Slicker." *(shakes his head)*

MISS DIANE: Never you mind, Cookie. Well, kids, *(to* SUZIE*)* we're just so proud you've joined us here at Bethlehem Gulch, aren't we boys?

DEAN: Sure thing, Miss D. I'm Dean and this is Doug. Say "howdy" to the youngins, Doug.

DOUG: "Howdy" to the youngins, Doug.

DEAN: Doug, quit horsin' around!

DOUG: I ain't horsin' around. I'm just sayin' what you told me ta say.

MISS DIANE: Hush, boys. Sometimes you ranch hands are a real burr in my saddle.

DEAN: Just doin' our job, ma'am. We pride ourselves to be the best sidekicks on the gulch.

COOKIE *(bows with his hat)*: I'm Cookie, and I'll be rustlin' up yur vittles.

DEAN: Tell 'em what kinda vittles Cookie!

COOKIE: Well, lemme see . . . I thought we'd have a little fried rattlesnake and some frog legs with a little rabbit stew. All fresh off the prairie. And finish things off with some sourdough butter biscuits.

*(*KIDS *frown at the thought.)*

MISS DIANE: Oh, youngins, Cookie's just messin' with y'all!

DEAN: Did you say butter biscuit? Cookie, I've been a smellin' some of your butter biscuits a coolin' in the chuck wagon. How 'bouts you sling one my way?

DOUG: Me, too! I'm as hungry as an 'ole bear.

COOKIE: You boys are always hungry. Now, hush! The grub is for the youngins. *(hits* DEAN *and* DOUG *with his hat)*

MISS DIANE: And who's that fellar over there standin' behind that tree with the sour pickle look on his face?

MITCH: Oh, that's Robert. He's my second cousin. He's staying with us for Christmas while his parents are out of town. I had to bring him! He wouldn't even wear cowboy stuff!

CASSIE: His Grandmother is very sick and his parents left him with Mitch's family to spend Christmas while they take care of her.

SUZIE: He told me on the bus ride up here that he's lonely and he misses his family.

MISS DIANE: Where abouts are his kinfolk?

MITCH: I think his grandparents live on the Big Island.

DOUG: I know that there place.

DEAN: Ya do?

DOUG: Yup, I went fishing there just yesterday. Caught me three big 'ole catfish.

COOKIE: No, Doug, the Big Island is over yonder in a place called Hawaii.

DOUG: Been there, too.

COOKIE: Now, when have you ever been to Hawaii?

DOUG: Why, me and Dean drove our 'ole pickup on Highway E last week to collect some can goods at the general store.

DEAN: Yep, he's got that right.

COOKIE: Now, hush! *(hits DEAN and DOUG with his hat)*

MISS DIANE *(walks to ROBERT and shakes his hand)*: Howdy, I'm Miss Diane.

ROBERT: I'm Robert C. Pigg from the New England Pigg Family.

DEAN: New England Pigg . . . I hear tell them there New England Pigg's are mighty tasty. *(rubs his stomach)*

DOUG: Yep, we'ins had a cook out behind the barn last week and I believe we roasted one of them there New England pigs. *(looks at ROBERT)* No resemblance, though.

MISS DIANE: Oh my, pay those boys no never mind, kids. How 'bout I call you Bobby?

ROBERT: If you don't mind, I think I prefer Robert.

CASSIE: Never mind him, Miss Diane. He's been grumpy all the way here.

MISS DIANE *(to ROBERT)*: Mitch told us that your Granny's a ailin', and that your Momma and Daddy are off tendin' to her. I know you must be a missin' them somethin' fierce.

ROBERT: No, I'll be fine. This is just not my idea of Christmas.

MISS DIANE: Well, Robert, we'll have you a smilin' before ya know it. I hope you kids are ready for some highfalutin fun out here in the gulch. We really know how to whoop it up, right boys?

DOUG & DEAN: Yippee! Ride em cowboy! Yee-haw!

(COOKIE looks at them and shakes his head and then in a lovin' way he pops them on the head with his hat because they won't stop hollering.)

COOKIE: Boys! *(raises his hat and DOUG and DEAN settle down)*

MISS DIANE: Cookie, you been feeding them boys too many jalapeñas again! Now, youngins grab a bail of hay or take a seat around the campfire. Let's us folks enjoy the Christmas lights.

MITCH: I don't see any lights, Miss D?

MISS DIANE: Look up, kids. The good Lord gave us the best light show you can ever see up there in His mighty heaven!

(Music begins)

Christmas Out Under the Stars

with
Away in a Manger

Words and Music by
PAM ANDREWS
Arr. by John DeVries

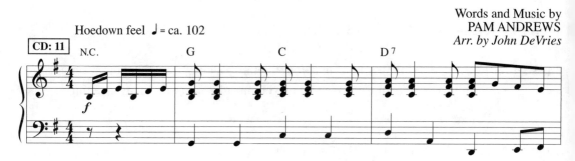

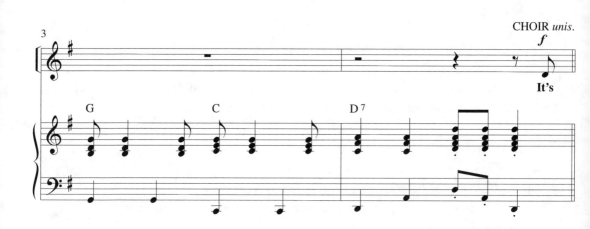

feel the joy___ down deep in-side,___ His love is in___ our hearts; So

bring on all the vit-tles, it's time we all___ should start; To

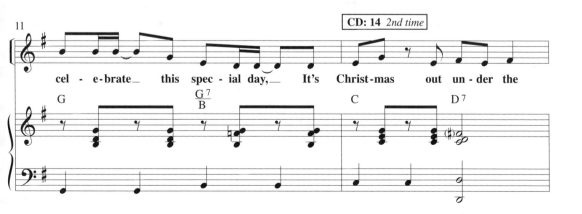

CD: 14 *2nd time*

cel - e-brate___ this spec - ial day,___ It's Christ-mas out un - der the

24

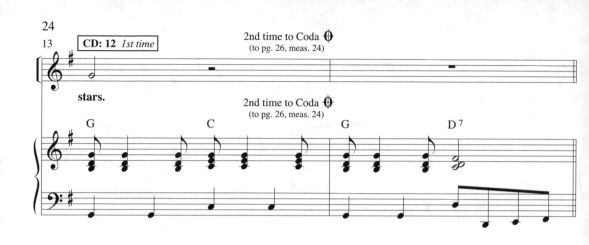

26

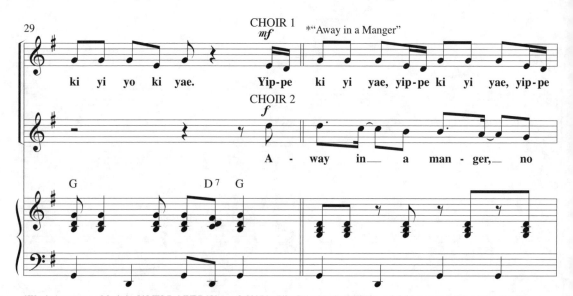

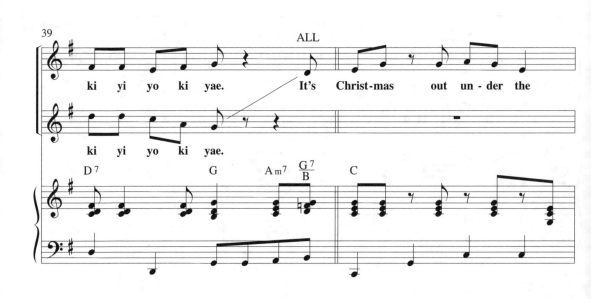

Scene 3

CASSIE: This is an awesome place, Miss Diane. The stars are so pretty.

SUZIE: "Twinkle, twinkle, little star, tells us Christmas is not far."

DOUG: Golly. You shore can spin a yarn, little lady.

DEAN: I can spin a yarn or two myself. "Twinkle, twinkle, little star, how I wonder what you are. You look like a big flashlight, make me want to say night-night!" *(snore)*

COOKIE: Put a cork in it, Dean.

MITCH: OK, enough with the stars . . . bring on the horses. I got these brand new boots so I can ride one of those big stallions.

SUZIE: Yeah, and I wanna see the cows.

DOUG: Uh-oh . . . here goes another customer.

DEAN: Yep. Better warm up the bus.

MISS DIANE: Land sakes, kids, I think you youngins have the wrong idea about Bethlehem Gulch.

DOUG: You're in a heap o' trouble, Miss Diane.

DEAN: Yup. A heap o' trouble.

SUZIE: What do you mean?

CASSIE: Yeah . . . this is a Christmas dude ranch, isn't it?

MISS DIANE: Yeah, you might say that, but we don't have horses and cows.

DEAN: Nope, you'll hear no mooooin' around here.

COOKIE: Not a steak on the premises.

DOUG: Nope. On this here ranch you only hear bayin', bayin', and more bayin'. This here's a sheep ranch.

ROBERT: Suzie! I thought you checked this place out.

SUZIE: The brochure said, "You'll have lots of heepin' fun at Bethlehem Gulch!"

DEAN: Look a little closer, little lady . . . it says, "You'll have lots of sheepin' fun at Bethlehem Gulch!"

DOUG (shaking his head): They never read that fine print.

MITCH: What a disaster!

CASSIE: I wore my cowgirl boots for nothing!

ROBERT (to MITCH): I told you this trip would be a disaster.

KIDS: We want our money back. Give us our money back!

MISS DIANE: Now, hold on there kids. This is really gonna be better than any horse or cattle ranch. You know, sheep and shepherds are a big part of the Christmas story.

MITCH: I know, Jesus, manger, sheep, shepherds . . . we know the story.

MISS DIANE: But don't you remember that sheep and shepherds were the first real visitors to Baby Jesus?

DEAN: Sounds like Miss Diane's fixin' to string you a Christmas yarn.

DOUG: I just love it when she tells about them there shepherds out in the fields nearby.

COOKIE: Yup, but that story always makes me cry. *(brings out a large handkerchief and blows his nose)*

MISS DIANE: Christmas is the story of the birth of our Lord Jesus, but it's also a great sheep tale.

DOUG: And she don't mean the swishy kind.

ROBERT: What a waste of time! I could be home playing my video games. Let's go!

MISS DIANE: How about you givin' Bethlehem Gulch a chance and if you don't like what I'm about to tell ya, I'll give your money back and you can pack up your gear and head for home.

MITCH: OK, I guess we can at least listen.

CASSIE: Yeah, let's give Miss Diane and Bethlehem Gulch a chance.

SUZIE: OK with you guys? *(motions to the CHOIR)*

CHOIR: Yep, let's do it. Let's give it a try. Yeah!

MISS DIANE: Great, kids. Well, the story I'm about to tell you is filled with wonder and amazement and joy.

COOKIE *(blows his nose)*: This one gets me right here. *(pounds his chest)*

MISS DIANE: It all began on a night like this . . . there were stars twinklin' in the sky. And near the town of Bethlehem, hunkered down for the night, was a small group of shepherds. Little did them there sheep boys know that this was a night . . . a special night . . . that the world would be changed forever.

(Music begins)

(SHEPHERDS enter during song.)

A Story of Shepherds

PAM ANDREWS
and NAHUM TATE

PAM ANDREWS
Arr. by John DeVries

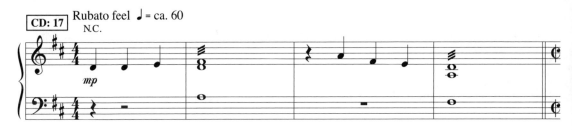

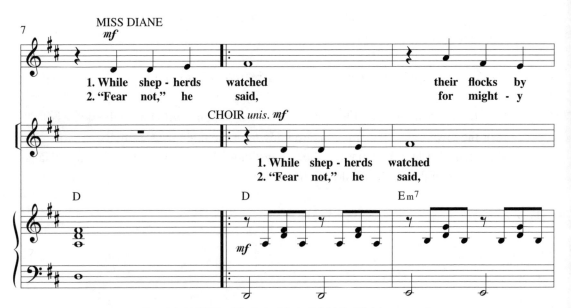

CD: 18 *1st time*

CD: 20 *2nd time*

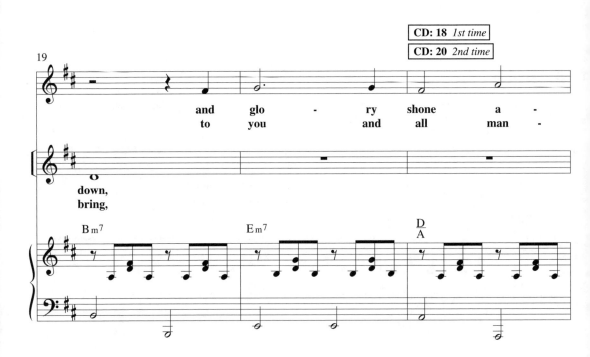

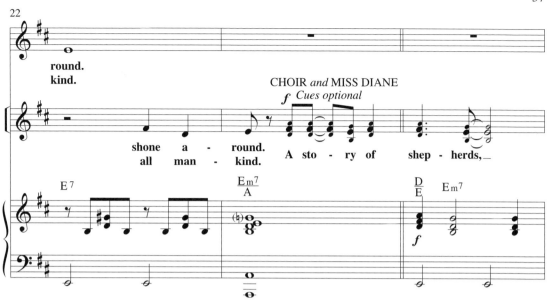

round.
kind.

shone a - round.
all man - kind.

CHOIR *and* MISS DIANE
f Cues optional

A sto - ry of shep - herds,—

way out___ on the plain,

Way out___ in the

des - ert,___

keep-in' watch night and day.

A sto - ry of shep - herds___ and an - gels on

B m7 · D/E · E m7 · A7

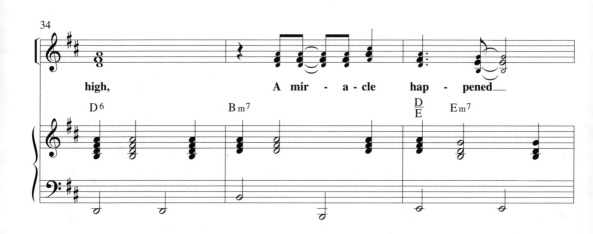

high, A mir - a - cle hap - pened___

D6 · B m7 · D/E · E m7

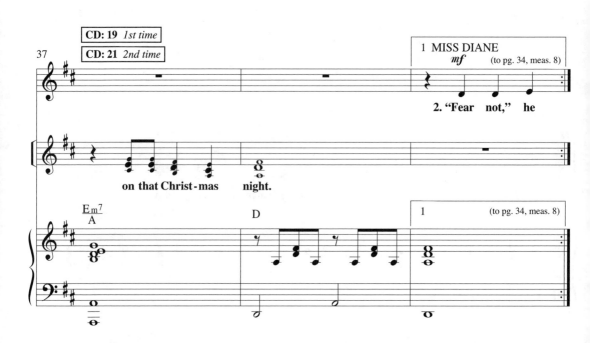

CD: 19 *1st time*
CD: 21 *2nd time*

1 MISS DIANE
mf (to pg. 34, meas. 8)

2. "Fear not," he

on that Christ - mas night.

E m7/A · D · 1 (to pg. 34, meas. 8)

Scene 4

MISS DIANE: Now, there were shepherds abidin' in their fields keepin' watch over their flocks by night . . .

(SHEPHERDS begin their dialogue.)

SPECK: Howdy, partner.

BUCK: Howdy, Speck.

SPECK: Hey, Buck, looks like we're pullin' the late watch again. Here we are . . . sheep boys on the midnight shift.

BUCK: Yup, and it's so borin' out here. All we got to do is hang out here on the prairie and hear sheep bayin' all night long.

SPECK: Yep, I brung me some pieces of bread to poke in my ears . . . then, maybe I can get me some shut-eye. By the way . . . who's the new kid over there?

BUCK: Dunno. Come on . . . let's go make his acquaintance. *(Walks to RORY)* Howdy, partner. Don't seem to remember seein' you around these parts before.

RORY: I'm Rory, and yep, this here's my first night out here on the range.

SPECK *(chuckles)*: Kind of scared are ya?

RORY: Naw. I'm fine. But . . . *(obviously scared)* is it always so dark out here?

BUCK: Partner . . . this ain't no dark night. The sky's full of them stars.

SPECK: Yup, them there stars should remind you that the Good Lord is watchin' over you.

BUCK: And anyway . . . you got us. We Bethlehem shepherds stick together.

SPECK: Through thick and thin.

BUCK: Yep, we sheep boys love our life on the range.

(Music begins)

Bethlehem Shepherds

Words and Music by
PAM ANDREWS
Arr. by John DeVries

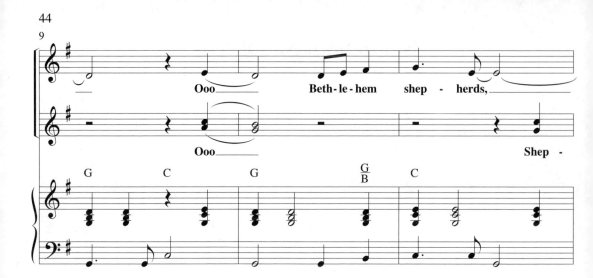

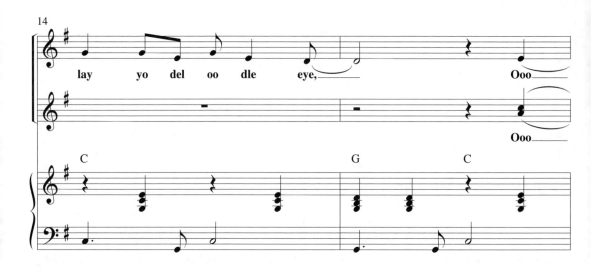

SHEPHERD 1 & 2

1. Peo - ple think___ we are lone - ly
2. We don't live___ ver - y swank - y,

C   G

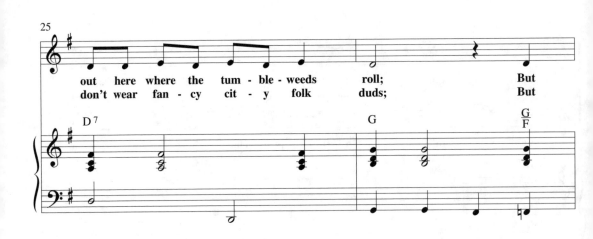

out here where the tum - ble - weeds roll; But
don't wear fan - cy cit - y folk duds; But

D7   G   G/F

CD: 25 *1st time*

CD: 27 *2nd time*

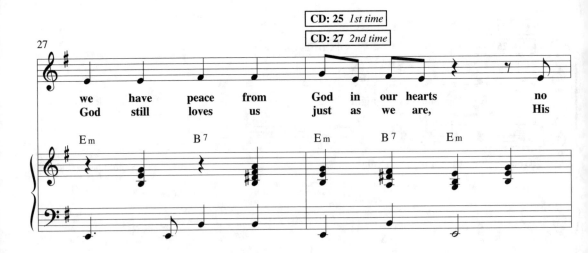

we have peace from God in our hearts no
God still loves us just as we are, His

Em   B7   Em   B7   Em

REPEAT TWICE
(to pg. 43, meas. 5)

mat - ter   where   we   roam.
light shines   down   on   us.

CHOIR *unis.*
mf

Beth - le - hem

REPEAT TWICE
(to pg. 43, meas. 5)

♦ CODA
SHEPHERD 3
mf

We   live   out____   in   the   des - ert

♦ CODA

tend - ing   to   our sheep wool - y   white;   But

48

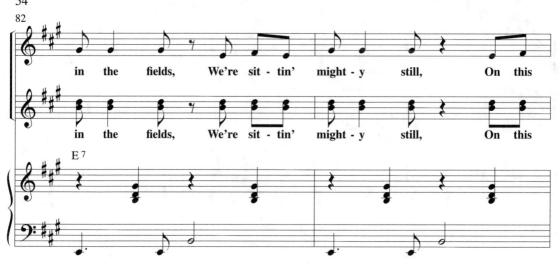

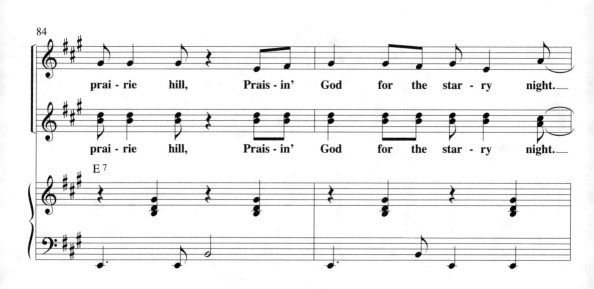

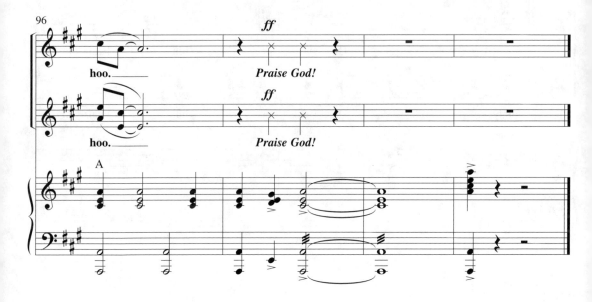

Scene 5

MISS DIANE: Now, them shepherds were a brave bunch of folks.

DOUG: I don't know about you all, but you wouldn't catch a fella like me out on that there range all alone.

DEAN: Doug, we are on the range and we are all alone.

DOUG: Don't tell me that, Dean. Haven't ya ever heard that ignorance is bliss?

COOKIE *(smiling)*: Then you two ought to be blissfully happy! *(hits them with his hat)*

CASSIE: Come on, Miss Diane. What happened next?

SUZIE: You know, Cassie . . . angels appeared.

MITCH: And they were afraid.

ROBERT: So they were alone . . . on Christmas?

MISS DIANE: Nope, not really, Robert.

ROBERT: But you said . . .

MISS DIANE: I know, but Robert when you're a member of the Good Lord's family, you're never alone. Them shepherds had God watchin over them that night. And the Good Lord has a bird's-eye view.

SUZIE: Come on, Miss Diane . . . what happened next?

DOUG: Tell 'em the part about the angels, Miss D.

DEAN: Yep, I love the part about them there angels.

COOKIE: Oh my, that part always makes me cry! *(cries)*

MISS DIANE: Well, now, something interestin' did happen next. I hear tell before the angels appeared those shepherds got in their bedrolls for some shut-eye.

(Scene shifts to SHEPHERDS)

SPECK: Don't know about you rascals, but I'm plum tired. I think I might catch me a few winks.

BUCK: Yep, the sheep are all bedded down. I'm sure we won't hear a peep out of them all night. No need to lose sleep watchin' sheep sleep.

RORY: You fellars think it's OK to catch some Z's?

SPECK: Shore thing, kid. Grab you a bedroll and curl up by the fire. We'll let Shep, our trusty sheepdog, keep an eye on these wooly wonders for a spell.

(SHEPHERDS curl up and go to sleep. SHEP howls.)

SHEEP 1: I thought they would never go to sleep. Humans are supposed to sleep better if they count sheep. If that's true, these shepherds should sleep for days!

SHEEP 2: Those humans talk and talk and talk. *(grabbing her head)* Makes my poor wooly headache.

SHEEP 3: How can they sleep like that? Don't they know a miracle is being born tonight?

SHEEP 4 *(sarcastically)*: Don't you remember . . . humans are always the last to know!

(Music begins)

Baa Baa Better Believe

Words and Music by
PAM ANDREWS
Arr. by John DeVries

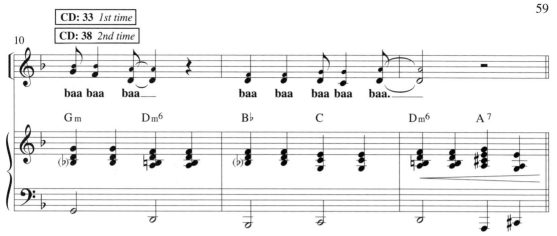

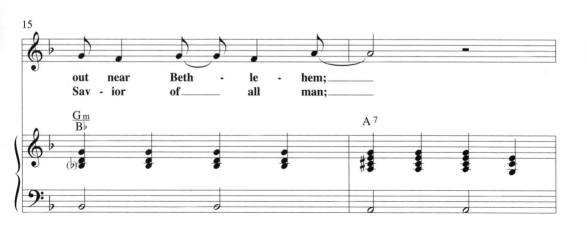

60

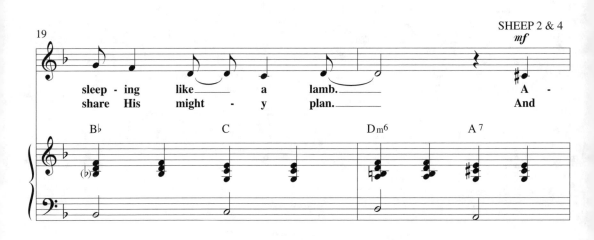

mir - a - cle's_____ at hand;_____ A
an - swer to_____ His call;_____ Yes,

CD: 35 *1st time*

CD: 40 *2nd time*

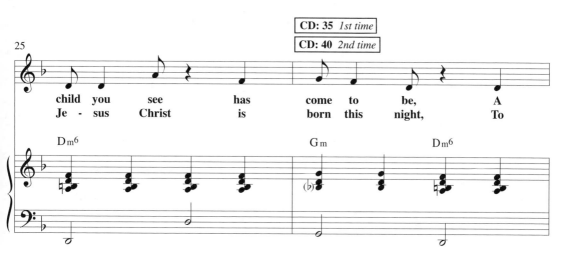

child you see has come to be, A
Je - sus Christ is born this night, To

Sav - ior for_____ all man._____
bring His light_____ to all._____

(to pg. 58, meas. 5)

66

Scene 6

(The SHEEP *lay down and pretend to sleep.* SHEP *howls.)*

BUCK: Speck, did you hear somethin'?

SPECK: Naw, you're hearin' things again, Buck. You must be dreamin' or that jelly sandwich ain't agreein' with you again.

BUCK: No, there ain't no denyin! I heard somethin', Speck. Take that there bread outta your ears and have a listen.

SPECK: Cut it out, Buck . . . you're scarin' the kid.

RORY *(nervously)*: I think I heard somethin', too. It kinda sounded like trumpets . . . like the ones they play in the king's court.

Shepherd's Fanfare

Music and Arrangement by
JOHN DEVRIES

BUCK *(obviously afraid)*: Speck, didn't you hear that?

SPECK *(obviously afraid)*: Yep, Buck, I'm hearin' somethin'.

RORY: Look! There's a light. Oh my, I'm shore afraid!

*(*SHEPHERDS *kneel and the* ANGELS *appear.)*

(Music begins)

This Is the Day of Our Savior's Birth

with

Angels We Have Heard on High

Words and Music by
PAM ANDREWS
Arr. by John DeVries

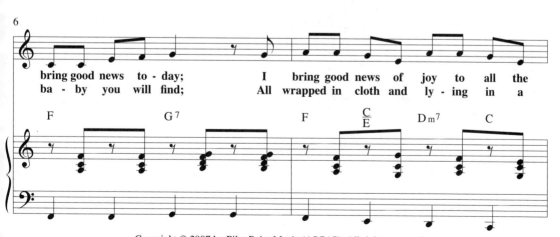

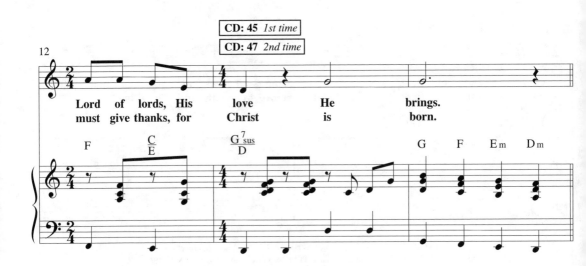

CHOIR

21

This is the day of our Sav - ior's birth.

This is the day of our Sav - ior's birth.

F   Dm   F   G   C

23

Glo - ry, glo - ry, to God in the high - est,

Glo - ry in the high, the high - est,

C   Am7   F   G7

25

Glo - ry, glo - ry, and peace on earth;

Glo - ry and peace on earth;

C   Am7   F   G7

*"Angels We Have Heard on High"

Scene 7

Shepherd's Fanfare

Music and Arrangement by
JOHN DEVRIES

(ANGELS *disappear*)

BUCK: Speck, in all my born days I ain't never seen anythin' like that!

RORY: Landsakes! This here weren't in my job description. I shore hope my insurance is up to date.

SPECK: Now, settle down, Rory. Didn't you hear them angels? They just told us about a miracle happenin' over yonder in Bethlehem. Way back long ago, them there prophets of old said, "For to us a child is born, to us a son is given, and the government will be on his shoulders. And he will be called Wonderful Counselor,

Mighty God, Everlasting Father, Prince of Peace."

BUCK: Now, that was beeeeutiful, Speck. Mighty purty if ya ask me.

SPECK: I know . . . some folks say I'm a songwriter at heart.

BUCK: I reckon you're right. Our Savior has been born and the angels come to tell us folks the good news.

SPECK: I don't know about you all, but I'm headin' to town. I wanna see what's a happenin', which them there angels told us about.

RORY: I'm right behind ya, Speck.

BUCK: Head 'em up and move 'em out! Let's blaze a trail to Bethlehem!

(SHEPHERDS *move to the manger scene.)*

MISS DIANE: Well, kids. Now, them shepherds weren't ones to waste precious time. As quick as lightnin' they was off to Bethlehem.

COOKIE *(blows his nose)*: This is the part that always makes me cry.

MISS DIANE: When them shepherds met up with Jesus, they just knelt right down and worshipped Him. Them shepherds knew He was special. They knew He was the Good Lord come to bring joy into this 'ole world.

(Music begins)

(SHEPHERDS *kneel before manger.)*

Gentle Shepherd

with
Savior, like a Shepherd Lead Us

GLORIA GAITHER and
WILLIAM J. GAITHER

WILLIAM J. GAITHER
Arr. by John DeVries

PLEASE NOTE: Copying of this product is NOT covered by CCLI licenses. For CCLI information call 1-800-234-2446.

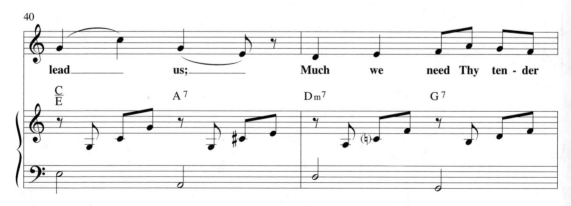

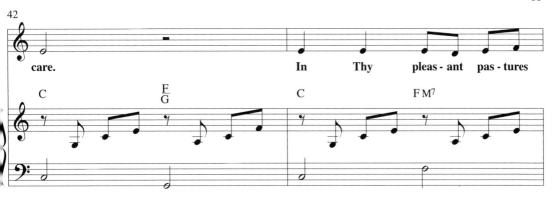

care. In Thy pleas-ant pas-tures

C | F/G | C | F M⁷

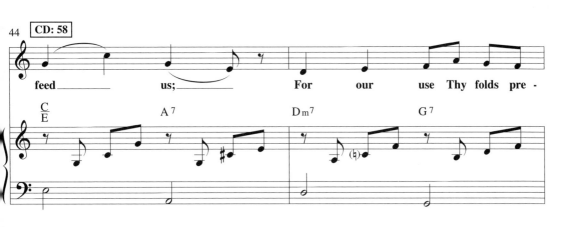

CD: 58

feed_____ us;_____ For our use Thy folds pre-

C/E | A⁷ | Dm⁷ | G⁷

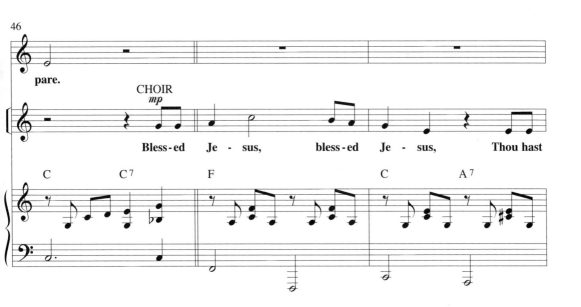

pare.

CHOIR
mp

Bless-ed Je - sus, bless-ed Je - sus, Thou hast

C | C⁷ | F | C | A⁷

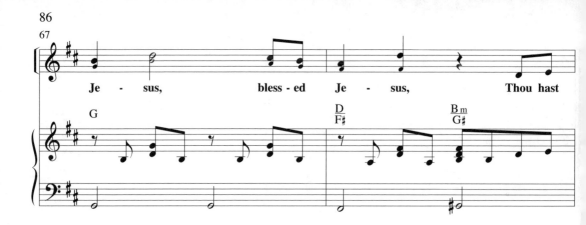

67

Je - sus, bless - ed Je - sus, Thou hast

G | D/F# | Bm/G#

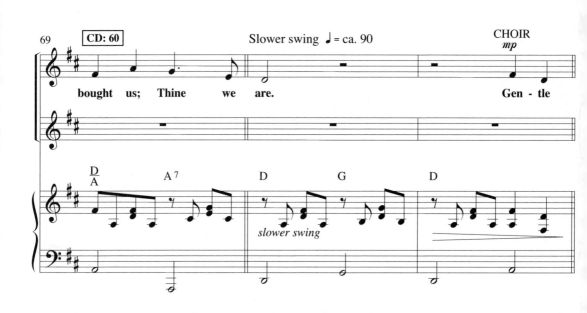

69 **CD: 60** Slower swing ♩ = ca. 90 CHOIR
mp

bought us; Thine we are. Gen - tle

D/A | A7 | D | G | D

slower swing

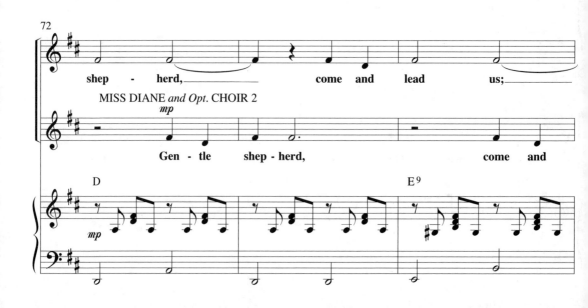

72

shep - herd, come and lead us;

MISS DIANE *and Opt.* CHOIR 2
mp

Gen - tle shep - herd, come and

D | | E9

mp

Scene 8

MISS DIANE: Now, kids, you might think them shepherds just went back to the pasture to
tend their sheep . . . but you'd be dead wrong.

MITCH: What did they do, Miss Diane?

SUZIE: Yes, finish the story.

CASSIE: What happened next?

DOUG: She's gettin' to the good part.

DEAN: You know, the time when . . .

COOKIE: Boys, hush. Don't give it away. Let Miss Diane finish up! *(hits* DOUG *and* DEAN *with his hat)*

MISS DIANE: Them sheep boys commenced a runnin' through town tellin' every soul they saw 'bout Baby Jesus. And you'll never guess, everyone . . . and I mean everyone, they told was simply amazed.

(The SHEPHERDS *rise from the manger scene and move to center stage. Children dressed in Biblical costumes should cross the stage and the* SHEPHERDS *speak to them.)*

SPECK *(stops some Bethlehem Townspeople)*: Howdy, partners! You folks won't believe what we here just saw!

BUCK: We met the one and only, true blue, tried and true King!

RORY: We lowly sheep boys just met Jesus!

(Music begins)

(The SHEPHERDS *move through the audience during this song randomly telling people that they just met the King.)*

We Just Met the King

Words and Music by
PAM ANDREWS
Arr. by John DeVries

(to pg. 89, meas. 9)

CHOIR *or opt. Small Group*

25

mf

1. Nev - er tho't that we would be, the
2. Je - sus lives in - side our hearts, and

Bb B C Db9

mf

28

ones to meet the Lord;___
He will al - ways stay;___

Loves us just the
There to love us,

Ab

Db9

CD: 63 *1st time*
CD: 65 *2nd time*

31

1,2 (to pg. 89, meas. 9)

way we are, He fills our hearts with joy.___
help us too, He's there to show the way.___

Db9 Bbm9 Bbm7

1,2
Eb7 Db/Eb

f

Scene 9

MITCH: That was an awesome story, Miss Diane.

MISS DIANE: Well, thanks, Mitch. The night our Good Lord came down to earth was a truly special occasion and really, youngins, things ain't ever been the same here on this 'ole earth.

ROBERT: Miss Diane, a while back you said something about being in the Lord's family. What did you mean?

, Robert, anyone who takes a hankerin' can be a part of the Lord's family. ...es some simple prayin', a lot of lovin, and then, folks can have Jesus livin' ...ir hearts for all time and eternity.

You, know, Miss Diane, I'm kinda like those shepherds alone this Christmas. My grandma's sick and my parents are away and I'm missing them.

MISS DIANE: Child, you've come to the right place. I know you're a missin' your Momma and Daddy. But, the best thing this 'ole gal can tell ya is that you have a Father up in heaven just waitin' to be with you every single minute.

ROBERT: You mean Jesus wants to know me?

MISS DIANE: Yup, He shore does. He can help you get through this troublesome time and make this bumpy trail you're a travelin' seem not quite as rough. You're one of His little lost sheep, Robert. He wants to help you find your way.

ROBERT: But, how can I know Jesus, Miss D? Isn't He far up in heaven?

MISS DIANE: The Good Lord is in heaven, but His Holy Spirit is right here just a waitin' to meet up with ya, Robert. Me and my 'ole sidekicks here would love to help you make your acquaintance with the Good Lord.

(DOUG, DEAN, and COOKIE nod their heads in agreement.)

ROBERT: Sounds great, Miss D. I'm so glad I'm here with you and *(gestures to everyone)* really all of you at Bethlehem Gulch. I may be missing my family, but you guys are showing me I have an even bigger family that loves me. By the way Miss D., you can call me Bobby.

(ROBERT hugs MISS DIANE)

COOKIE: Now, cut that out, Miss D. You know, that sentimental stuff always makes me cry. *(blows his nose)*

MITCH: Look, Miss Diane, Bobby is smiling. You said we'd all be smiling if we stayed here on the sheep ranch with you and you were right!

CASSIE: Yep! We're having a highfalutin' good time!

SUZIE *(in a country voice)*: We shore are! We all want to stay, right everybody?

CHOIR: Yes!!! We want to stay!!! Yee-haw!!!

MISS DIANE: My, my, y'all are such sweet little lambs. All right, youngins, I think it's time we head on out to the range. Cookie, you got some grub for us to eat out on the trail

COOKIE: Yes, ma'am, Miss Diane. I even whipped up a little 'ole birthday cake for the occasion! *(Brings out a birthday cake with candles from the chuck wagon)*

DEAN: Yee-haw! Birthday cake!

DOUG: I'm as hungry as an 'ole mountain lion!

COOKIE: Ain't there a livin' breathin' animal you ain't hungry as?

DOUG: Well, I ain't hungry as a bird.

COOKIE: You boys get on my last nerve! *(starts to hit them with his hat, but instead puts it on his head, then grins)*

DOUG: Well, doggies! Even Cookie's got the Christmas spirit.

DEAN: Yep, Christmas is shorely here at Bethlehem Gulch!

MISS DIANE: Well, grab your coats and let's go tend some sheep!

(MAIN CAST exits)

KID 1: Do you know the Great Shepherd? Jesus came to earth to save us, love us, and help us. This Christmas, make Him the Shepherd of your life. Jesus said in John 10:11, "I am the good shepherd. The good shepherd lays down his life for the sheep." Ask Jesus to come into your heart to live forever. Then, do just as the shepherds did and tell others about Jesus this Christmas. Sharing the joy of knowing Jesus is the best gift you can ever give.

(Music begins)

Christmas at Bethlehem Gulch Finale

includes

Come, Thou Long-expected Jesus
Our Great Savior
Go, Tell It on the Mountain
Christmas at Bethlehem Gulch

Arr. by John DeVries
"Come, Thou Long-expected Jesus"

100

CD: **72** *1st time*
CD: **74** *2nd time*

62

moun - tain That Je - sus Christ is born! He is

F   B♭   F/C   C   F

65   SOLO
          mf

born! He is born!

1. While
2. The

F m⁷   Gm/F   F m⁷   Gm/F

67

shep - herds kept their watch - ing O'er
shep - herds feared and trem - bled When

F

mf

si - lent flocks___ by___ night, Be -
lo! a - bove___ the___ earth Rang

C   F

hold! through - out___ the heav - ens There
out the an - gel cho - rus That

F

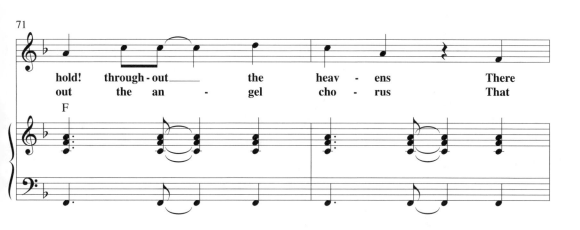

CD: 73 1st time
CD: 75 2nd time

shone a ho - ly light.
hailed our Sav - ior's birth.

mf cresc.

Ho - ly light,___ ho - ly light.
Ho - ly birth,___ ho - ly birth.

G   C 7

cresc.

CD: 76

*"Christmas at Bethlehem Gulch"

93

yee - haw! Wel - come, wel - come,

in you'll have a ball.___ Wel - come, wel - come, you'll

F7   Bb

95

come on in!

find that Christ-mas touch, Come right on in___ and join the fun,___ it's

Eb   E°7   Bb/F   G7

97

One more time!

Christ-mas at Beth - le - hem Gulch. Come

Cm7   F7   Bb

Christmas at Bethlehem Gulch Curtain Call

includes
Go, Tell It on the Mountain
Christmas at Bethlehem Gulch

Arr. by John DeVries

*"Go, Tell It on the Mountain"

Hoedown feel ♩ = ca. 123

*"Christmas at Bethlehem Gulch"
SMALL GROUP

Wel-come, wel-come,

CHOIR *unis.*

Wel-come, wel-come,

how-dy! Wel-come,

how-dy one and all;___ Wel-come, wel-come, come right

PRODUCTION NOTES

Setting

The setting should be very simple.

Bethlehem Gulch - The Bethlehem Gulch scene should be center stage. You may want to create a barn flat with a split rail fence. You could have bails of straw, saw horses, lariats, tumble weeds (made from rolled grapevine) or anything that might make the set look western. You could even have a chuck wagon. Remember to stay with the old west prairie look. Keep things simple. There is a backdrop design provided for you in the "Christmas at Bethlehem Gulch Resource Notebook" and complete construction ideas on the "Christmas at Bethlehem Gulch DVD Resource." Art can also be retrieved from the Lillenas website. You will also want to have stars in the sky. These can happen on the backdrop, be web lights, or you could have the children pretend they see lights.

Shepherd Scene - For the shepherd scene you may want to continue with the prairie look adding possibly a cactus to the tumbleweeds and maybe a watering hole. Again, the sky should be dark with stars if possible.

Manger Scene - The manger scene should be a traditional manger scene. Mary, Joseph around a manger with a doll wrapped in cloth. You could add an actual stable with children in animal costumes or keep things simple with only the manger. Again, keep the night-time feel going with stars and possibly a larger star over the manger scene.

Casting Ideas

Do you have a large, middle-sized, or small choir? Don't worry, this musical is perfect for any size choir. You may do the musical as written utilizing only the main characters if you have a smaller choir. If your choir is large, you may want to divide parts, or add solos. Be creative. Give everyone a part if possible. Giving every child some kind of special part will encourage attendance and participation. Pray and God will lead you to the right decisions.

Cast

Miss Diane	_____	Doug	_____
Dean	_____	Cookie	_____
Robert	_____	Cassie	_____
Mitch	_____	Suzie	_____
Speck	_____	Buck	_____
Rory	_____	Shep	_____

Angels (Solos - non-speaking)

Angel 1	_____	Angel 2	_____
Angel 3	_____	Angel 4	_____
Sheep 1	_____	Sheep 2	_____
Sheep 3	_____	Sheep 4	_____

Mary (non-speaking) _____

Joseph (non-speaking) _____

Kid 1 _____

Specialty Dancers

To move or not to move?

In an effort to supply the needs of all our churches, we are providing you with choreography for this children's choir musical. We realize that according to various denominations, this may or may not be appropriate for your church. We encourage you to seek the leadership of your church and seek the Lord in prayer as you make your decision. God bless YOU and know we are always here for questions or comments.

Note: The movement for the Specialty Dances as well as a complete list of movement props are found in the "Christmas at Bethlehem Gulch Resource Notebook" or on the "Christmas at Bethlehem Gulch DVD."

"Christmas at Bethlehem Gulch" Movement Teams

_____	_____
_____	_____
_____	_____
_____	_____
_____	_____
_____	_____
_____	_____
_____	_____

Movement Props

Song 1: Christmas at Bethlehem Gulch
     Prop - Hats & Bandanas
     Alt. prop - Welcome Signs, Wooden Spoons & Buckets

Song 2: Christmas Out Under the Stars
     Prop - Silver Stars
     Alt. prop - Sheep costume & Star Gloves

Song 3: A Story of Shepherds
     Prop - Cowboy hats & Bandanas
     Alt. prop - Lariats

Song 4: Bethlehem Shepherds
     Prop - Mustaches & Cowboy Costumes
     Alt. prop - Shepherd's Staves

Song 5: Baa Baa Better Believe
     Prop - Sheep Gloves & Ears
     Alt. prop - Sheep Costumes

Song 6: This Is the Day of Our Savior's Birth
     Prop - Wagon Wheel Tambourines
     Alt. prop - Angel Streamers

Song 7: Gentle Shepherd
     Prop - Bandanas & Cowboy Hats
     Alt. prop - Jesus Stars

Song 8: We Just Met the King
     Prop - Bandana Wrist Bands
     Alt. prop - "THE KING" Sign

Song 9: Christmas at Bethlehem Gulch Finale
     Prop - None
     Alt. prop - Bandana Shakers

Cast and Costume

Miss Diane - Miss Diane could wear any type of western wear. Cowboy hat, boots, bandana, denim skirt or jeans would be fine.

Doug - Doug could wear any type western wear. Cowboy hat, boots, bandana, and jeans would be fine. You may want to add a vest. Doug should look like a rough and ready cowboy. Try to make Doug look different from Dean . . . different bandana color would be great. You could also have Doug wear the Bethlehem Gulch T-shirt, jeans, bandana, and vest.

Dean - Dean could wear any type western wear. Cowboy hat, boots, bandana, and jeans would be fine. You may want to add a vest. Dean should look like a rough and ready cowboy. Try to make Dean look different from Doug . . . different bandana color would be great. You could also have Dean wear the Bethlehem Gulch T-shirt, jeans, bandana, and vest.

Cookie - Cookie should be dressed in cowboy gear like Dean and Doug. Cowboy hat, boots, bandana, and jeans would be fine. Cookie can be a boy or a girl so you may want to dress Cookie in jeans or a jeans skirt depending on your casting choice. To finish Cookie's look, you should add an apron. He/She could even wear a chef's hat if you like.

Robert - Robert should wear preppy clothes. He could still look western . . . just refined western.

Cassie, Mitch, and Suzie - Cassie, Mitch, and Suzie should wear a Bethlehem Gulch T-shirt, jeans, bandana, cowboy hat, and boots.

Speck, Buck, and Rory (Shepherds 1, 2, and 3) - Speck should wear biblical clothes which portray the shepherd look, but add a cowboy hat and boots. You may want to add a lariat for a belt. Make each shepherd look unique.

Shep - Shep should wear a dog costume. You could purchase this costume at your local costume shop, or create the dog look by having the child wear a brown or white running suit with painted-on spots. You would then want to add ears.

Angels - The Angels should wear biblical clothes which portray the angel look, but add a white cowboy hat and white boots. (Remember, you can purchase boots at your local thrift store and spray paint them white.) Also, you would want to add wings and a halo. The wings can be purchased at a costume novelty shop or made by stretching netting over hangers shaped as wings. The halo could simply be a circle of gold or silver Christmas garland. You may also want to add garland rings for movement.

The rings can be made by wrapping an embroidery hoop with gold or silver garland and tapping into place.

Sheep 1, 2, 3, & 4 - The sheep should wear a sheep costume. You could purchase this costume at your local costume shop, or create the sheep look by having the child wear a white or black running suit with a vest of glued on quilt batting. You would then want to add ears. Also, you could make paws from socks with glued on quilt batting.

Mary - Mary should wear a blue biblical costume

Joseph - Joseph should wear a brown biblical costume

Kid 1 - Kid 1 should wear the Bethlehem Gulch T-shirt and jeans.

Additional Animals - You could add sheep for the shepherd scene. Another area where animals could be added is in the depiction of the manger.

Choir - The Choir speaking parts should wear the Bethlehem Gulch T-shirt and jeans.

To purchase these T-shirts, contact: Personalized Gifts & Appareal
Tom Roland, Owner
(888) 898-6172
Website: www.pg4u.com
E-mail: info@pg4u.com
OR you can download the T-shirt art at the Lillenas website www.lillenaskids.com to create your own shirt.

Set Design

The following is the layout of the set.

Bethlehem Gulch Backdrop
Risers

Bethlehem Gulch Set

Shepherd Scene   Nativity

Soloists   Soloists
X X   X X

Props

<table>
<tr><td>Pretend fire</td><td>Rustic pots and pans</td></tr>
<tr><td>Iron skillets</td><td>Rustic cooking spoons</td></tr>
<tr><td>Rustic plates, forks, and spoons</td><td>Pretend school bus (Optional)</td></tr>
<tr><td>Hay bales</td><td>Stumps</td></tr>
<tr><td>Biscuits</td><td>Tree</td></tr>
<tr><td>3-4 Handkerchiefs</td><td>3 Shepherd's staves</td></tr>
<tr><td>Loaf of bread</td><td>Jelly sandwich (Optional)</td></tr>
<tr><td>Manger</td><td>Birthday cake and candles</td></tr>
</table>

Specialty Dancers

The Specialty Dancer costuming is found in the "Christmas at Bethlehem Gulch Resource Notebook" or displayed on the "Christmas at Bethlehem Gulch DVD."

Solos

Please Note: The Optional "Small Groups" are mini choirs you can pull from your choir. They can learn harmony and echoes. This feature provides a means for more parts for your choir.

Christmas at Bethlehem Gulch Overture	No Solo
Christmas at Bethlehem Gulch	Miss Diane, Optional Small Group
Christmas Out Under the Stars	No Solo, Optional Small Group
A Story of Shepherds	Miss Diane, Optional Small Group
Bethlehem Shepherds	Speck, Buck, Rory, Optional Small Group
Baa Baa Better Believe	4 Sheep, Optional Small Group
This Is the Day of Our Savior's Birth	Angel Solo 1, Angel Solo 2, Choir 1 & Choir 2
Gentle Shepherd	Solo with Miss Diane, Opt. Small Group Solo, Optional Small Group
We Just Met the King	Optional Small Group
Christmas at Bethlehem Gulch Finale	2 Solos, Optional Small Group
Christmas at Bethlehem Gulch Curtain Call	No Solo

Microphone Needs

It would be good to have a cordless lavaliere microphone for each main character. Handheld microphones can be used as a substitute. Place two solo microphones on stands stage left and stage right to accommodate the solos.

Scripture References
(All references NIV)

Christmas at Bethlehem Gulch Overture

Isaiah 9:6 - For to us a child is born, to us a son is given, and the government will be on his shoulders. And he will be called Wonderful Counselor, Mighty God, Everlasting Father, Prince of Peace.

Song 1 - Christmas at Bethlehem Gulch

Matthew 1:21 - She will give birth to a son, and you are to give him the name Jesus, because he will save his people from their sins.

Song 2 - Christmas Out Under the Stars

Matthew 2:10 - When they saw the star, they were overjoyed.

Song 3 - A Story of Shepherds

Luke 2:8 - And there were shepherds living out in the fields nearby, keeping watch over their flocks at night.

Song 4 - Bethlehem Shepherds

Luke 2:11 - Today in the town of David a Savior has been born to you; he is Christ the Lord.

Song 5 - Baa Baa Better Believe

John 6:69 - We believe and know that you are the Holy One of God.

Song 6 - This Is the Day of Our Savior's Birth

Luke 2:14 - Glory to God in the highest, and on earth peace to men on whom his favor rests.

Song 7 - Gentle Shepherd

John 10:11 - I am the good shepherd. The good shepherd lays down his life for the sheep.

Song 8 - We Just Met the King

Luke 2:17-18 - When they had seen him, they spread the word concerning what had been told them about this child, and all who heard it were amazed at what the shepherds said to them.

Song 9 - Christmas at Bethlehem Gulch Finale

Haggai 2:7 - And the desired of all nations will come, and I will fill this house with glory, says the LORD Almighty.

Matthew 28:18-20 - Then Jesus came to them and said, "All authority in heaven and on earth has been given to me. Therefore go and make disciples of all nations, baptizing them in the name of the Father and of the Son and of the Holy Spirit, and teaching them to obey everything I have commanded you. And surely I am with you always, to the very end of the age."

Christmas at Bethlehem Gulch Curtain Call

Isaiah 53:6 - We all, like sheep, have gone astray, each of us has turned to his own way; and the LORD has laid on him the iniquity of us all.

Christmas
at
Bethlehem
GULCH

Christmas
at
Bethlehem
GULCH

Christmas
at
Bethlehem
GULCH